Cinderella

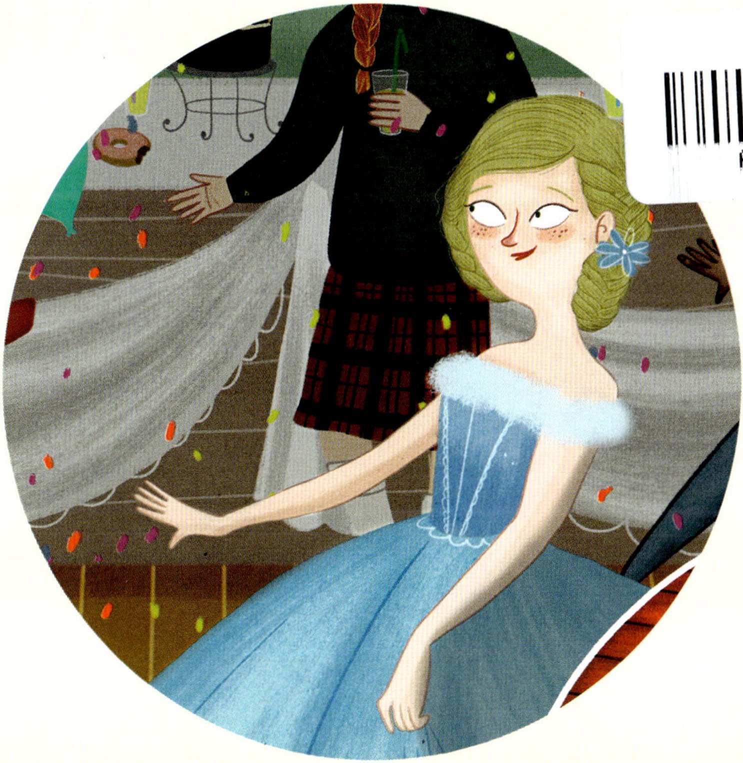

Written by Gill Budgell

Illustrated by Beatriz Castro

RISING STARS

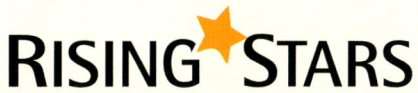

sad

zap

tick-tock

bad luck

cross

Talk about the story

Ask your child these questions:

1. What was Cinderella doing at the start of the book?
2. What did the fairy do with her magic?
3. Why did Cinderella lose her shoe?
4. Why were the sisters cross?
5. Do you like going to parties? Why/Why not?
6. Have you ever lost something? What did you lose?

Can your child retell the story using their own words?